W9-BLB-245

LE CORDON BLEU

HOME COLLECTION

·FINGER FOOD·

PERIPLUS

contents

recipe ratings ✴ *easy* ✴✴ *a little more care needed* ✴✴✴ *more care needed*

Salmon, shrimp and avocado rolls

These rolls are extremely simple to prepare and require no cooking. To ensure excellent results, the ingredients must be of the finest quality.

Preparation time **25 minutes**
Total cooking time **None**
Makes 32

10 oz. smoked salmon slices
1/2 avocado
1 tablespoon lemon juice
16 medium cooked shrimp, shelled and deveined
lumpfish roe, to garnish
fresh dill weed, to garnish

1 Cut the salmon slices into 2- x 1 1/4-inch rectangles. Remove the pit from the avocado half, cut in two and remove the skin. Then cut each quarter into four or five slices lengthwise and cut the slices in half through the middle. Place the pieces in a bowl and toss in the lemon juice.
2 Roll a piece of avocado or a shrimp in each piece of salmon and place on a serving tray. Decorate the rolls with some lumpfish roe and a sprig of dill weed.

Chef's tip These rolls can be prepared several hours in advance. Once assembled, cover with plastic wrap and store in the refrigerator.

Cheese-stuffed mushrooms

These firm raw mushrooms with a soft mixed herb and garlic cream cheese filling are easy to prepare and delicious to eat. If making large quantities, it is quicker to use a pastry bag to fill the mushrooms.

Preparation time **20 minutes**
Total cooking time **5 minutes**
Makes about 20

20 evenly sized button mushrooms
1 small clove garlic, halved
1/2 cup cream cheese
2 tablespoons chopped mixed fresh herbs, such as
  parsley, chives and thyme
1 teaspoon lemon juice
chopped fresh garlic chives or fresh chervil or parsley
  leaves, to garnish

1 Remove any dirt from the mushrooms with your fingers and lightly wipe with a clean soft towel to remove any remaining dirt. Cut the stems from the mushrooms and discard.

2 Put the garlic halves into a small saucepan and cover with water. Bring to a boil, simmer for 3 minutes, then drain. Crush the garlic and put into a small bowl. Add the cream cheese, mixed herbs and lemon juice and mix together until smooth. Season generously with salt and freshly ground black pepper.

3 Spoon the filling into a pastry bag fitted with a small star nozzle and pipe into each mushroom. Alternatively, use a teaspoon to fill each mushroom with the cheese and herb mixture until it comes slightly over the top of the mushroom.

4 Arrange the stuffed mushrooms on a serving dish, cover loosely with plastic wrap and chill until ready to serve. Each mushroom can be decorated with either a sprinkling of chopped garlic chives or a small leaf of chervil or parsley. Alternatively, you could decorate the mushrooms with a small diamond-shaped piece of tomato to add color.

Chicken liver pâté

A simply made pâté dip with lots of flavor. If you want a stronger flavor, try making it with duck livers.

*Preparation time **15 minutes** + **15 minutes cooling***
*Total cooking time **10 minutes***
Serves 4 as an appetizer

1/2 cup unsalted butter, at room temperature
2 shallots, finely chopped
2 cloves garlic, finely chopped
8 oz. chicken livers, trimmed
sprig of fresh thyme
bay leaf
large pinch each of ground nutmeg, cloves and cinnamon
1 tablespoon brandy or port
2 tablespoons whipping cream or crème fraîche

1 Place 2 tablespoons of the butter in a skillet and add the shallots and garlic. Cook over a gentle heat until they soften and turn transparent.
2 Over medium heat, add the livers, thyme, bay leaf, spices and some salt and pepper to the shallot mixture. Fry for 3 minutes. The livers should be barely pink in the center. Set aside to cool for 15 minutes.
3 Remove the thyme and bay leaf from the mixture and process in a food processor until smooth, then push through a sieve if you prefer an even smoother texture. Beat in the remaining butter using a wooden spoon, then add the brandy or port. Carefully fold in the cream or crème fraîche and season to taste with salt and freshly ground black pepper. Spoon into a serving bowl and serve with Melba toast or toasted bread fingers.

Chef's tip If prepared in advance and refrigerated, the pâté may be too firm to be eaten as a dip straight from the refrigerator. Allow to soften for about 30 minutes at room temperature before serving.

Salmon rillettes

This modern version of the classic French meat rillettes—similar to pâté—uses both fresh and smoked salmon.

*Preparation time **10 minutes** + **1 hour chilling***
*Total cooking time **10 minutes***
Serves 4 as an appetizer

4 oz. salmon fillet, skinned and boned
2 oz. smoked salmon slices, finely chopped
1/3 cup unsalted butter, at room temperature
1/4 cup plain yogurt
1 teaspoon lemon juice
2 tablespoons chopped fresh chives

1 Steam the fresh salmon for 8–10 minutes, or until cooked through. Cool on a clean towel or several pieces of paper towel.
2 Using a whisk or fork, mix the smoked salmon with the butter until as smooth as possible. Add the yogurt, lemon juice and chives. Mix until well combined, season to taste and set aside.
3 Gently crush the fresh salmon to make large flakes and add to the smoked salmon mixture. Mix until completely incorporated. Transfer to a small serving bowl or terrine and refrigerate for 1 hour, or until set. Serve with Melba toast or French bread.

Chef's tip You can also make a mackerel rillette by replacing the fresh salmon with three or four skinned and boned fresh mackerel fillets, about 4 oz. Replace the smoked salmon with the same quantity of smoked mackerel and substitute lime juice for the lemon juice.

Chicken liver pâté (top) and Salmon rillettes

Mini spring rolls

The mouth-watering combination of vegetables cooked with soy sauce, ginger, garlic and sesame seeds, enclosed in crisp golden brown phyllo pastry, makes these spring rolls a real treat. This recipe does not require a deep-fat fryer as the spring rolls are cooked in the oven.

Preparation time **40 minutes + 15 minutes cooling**
Total cooking time **15 minutes**
Makes 45

2/3 cup unsalted butter, melted
3 tablespoons sesame oil
5 cups mixed vegetables julienne, such as leek,
carrot, rutabaga, bean sprouts, snow peas
and celery root (see Chef's tips)
I tablespoon chopped scallion
I-inch piece fresh ginger root, finely chopped
I clove garlic, finely chopped
2 tablespoons sesame seeds, toasted (see Chef's tips)
I tablespoon soy sauce
10 phyllo pastry sheets

1 Brush two baking sheets with a little melted butter and set aside.

2 Heat the sesame oil in a skillet until smoking, then add the vegetables julienne and scallion and cook for 2 minutes, stirring constantly. Stir in the ginger, garlic, sesame seeds and soy sauce and cook for another 1 minute. Season to taste and turn the vegetable mixture out onto a plate to cool completely.

3 Preheat the oven to 400°F. Following the method in the Chef's techniques on page 63, lay a sheet of phyllo pastry on a work surface and brush one side with melted butter. Lay a second sheet on top of the buttered side and brush with more melted butter. Repeat to produce five stacks, each with two layers of phyllo. Cut each stack into nine rectangles, each measuring about 6 x 3 1/2 inches. Spoon an equal amount of filling onto the short end of each rectangle, leaving 1/2 inch free of filling on either side. Turn the sides in and roll up tightly to enclose the filling.

4 Place the rolls onto the prepared baking sheets, brush with melted butter and bake in the oven for about 10–12 minutes, or until golden and crisp. Serve the spring rolls immediately, with some soy or sweet chili sauce if desired.

Chef's tips Julienne strips are even-size strips of vegetables the size and shape of matchsticks.
To toast the sesame seeds, place on a baking sheet and bake in a 350°F oven for 4–5 minutes, or until golden brown. Alternatively, you can place them in a small, dry skillet and stir over medium heat until golden brown. Remove from the pan immediately and set aside to allow to cool.

Onion tartlets

These delectable golden onion tartlets must be served warm. The onion filling can be replaced with a mushroom filling, as described in the chef's tip below. If short of time, you could use pre-rolled sheets of frozen puff pastry.

Preparation time **45 minutes +35 minutes chilling**
Total cooking time **45 minutes**
Makes 24

PASTRY
1²/3 cups all-purpose flour
1/4 teaspoon salt
3 tablespoons unsalted butter, cut up
2 egg yolks
4–5 tablespoons water

ONION FILLING
2 tablespoons unsalted butter
2 onions, finely chopped
1 small bay leaf
2 sprigs of fresh thyme

2/3 cup whipping cream
4 eggs
4 egg yolks
pinch of ground nutmeg

1 Butter 24 individual mini tartlet pans or 24 mini muffin cups.
2 To make the pastry, sift together the flour and salt into a large bowl. Using your fingertips, rub in the butter until the flour is evenly colored and sandy in texture. Make a well in the center and add the egg yolks and water. Mix well, form into a ball and cover with plastic wrap. Place in the refrigerator to chill for about 20 minutes.
3 To make the onion filling, melt the butter in a skillet over medium heat. Add the onions, bay leaf and thyme with a pinch of salt. Cover and cook slowly for 15 minutes, then remove the cover and continue to cook for about 15 minutes, or until the onions are dark golden in color. Remove the bay leaf and thyme and cool.
4 Roll out the dough to a thickness of 1/8 inch, then refrigerate for 5 minutes. Preheat the oven to 350°F. Using a round cutter slightly larger than the tartlet pans, cut out 24 rounds. Place the rounds in each pan, pressing down on the bottom so that the dough extends slightly above the edges. Place in the refrigerator to chill for 10 minutes. Whisk together the cream, eggs, egg yolks, nutmeg and salt and freshly ground black pepper.
5 Divide the onion filling among the tartlet shells, then cover with the egg mixture. Bake for 12–15 minutes, or until lightly browned. Remove from the pans while still warm and serve immediately.

Chef's tip If you want to replace the onion with a mushroom filling, melt 2 tablespoons butter in a saucepan over medium heat, add 3 finely chopped shallots and cook for about 3 minutes. Toss 2 1/2 cups finely chopped mushrooms in 1 tablespoon lemon juice, add to the shallots and cook for another 10 minutes, or until dry. Set the filling aside to cool.

Pronto puff pizzas

Simply the quickest, crispiest and most delicious pizzas you'll ever make—these Pronto puffs are just ideal for the busy entertainer.

Preparation time **20 minutes**
Total cooking time **20 minutes**
Makes about 20

1 sheet pre-rolled frozen puff pastry, thawed
1 egg, beaten
1 small yellow bell pepper
1 small red bell pepper
1 zucchini, halved lengthwise
2–3 tomatoes, thinly sliced
4 artichoke hearts, drained and cut
  into 1/2-inch cubes
3 oz. mozzarella cheese, cut into 1/2-inch cubes
1 teaspoon dried mixed herbs

1 Place the pastry on a baking sheet and brush with the egg. Set aside in the refrigerator.

2 To broil the peppers, follow the method in the Chef's techniques on page 62. Add the zucchini, skin-side-up, to the preheated broiler a little after the peppers, and also broil until the skin has blackened, but do not peel.

3 Preheat the oven to 400°F. Slice the zucchini into 1/4-inch-thick semicircles. Cut the peeled peppers into 1/4-inch strips.

4 Using a 2-inch plain round cutter, cut circles from the pastry and place on two lightly greased baking sheets. Top with a slice of tomato, a strip of yellow and red pepper, some artichoke and zucchini, and a few cubes of mozzarella, then sprinkle lightly with the herbs. Bake in the oven for 8–10 minutes, or until puffed and lightly browned.

Spinach and feta parcels

*These delicious small parcels, resembling purses, have a lovely crisp exterior
and a soft creamy center.*

Preparation time 30 minutes + 15 minutes cooling
Total cooking time 20 minutes
Makes about 45

1/3 cup unsalted butter, melted
1 tablespoon olive oil
6 1/4 cups spinach, washed, trimmed and torn
3/4 cup crumbled feta cheese
1/4 cup ricotta or small-curd cottage cheese
1 egg, beaten
1 tablespoon chopped fresh parsley
1 tablespoon chopped fresh basil
6 sheets phyllo pastry

1 Brush two baking sheets with melted butter.
2 Heat the oil in a skillet. Add the spinach and cook for 2 minutes, stirring constantly. Stir in the feta and ricotta until they become soft and coat the spinach. Season to taste with salt and freshly ground black pepper. Remove the pan from the heat, cool slightly, then stir in the egg, parsley and basil. Set aside for about 15 minutes to cool completely.

3 Preheat the oven to 375°F. Following the method in the Chef's techniques on page 63, lay a sheet of phyllo pastry flat on a work surface and brush one side with melted butter. Lay a second sheet on top and brush with more melted butter. Repeat to produce three stacks, each with two layers of phyllo. Cut each stack into 3-inch squares, discarding any leftover pastry. Put 1 teaspoon of filling in the center of a square, then gather up the corners over the filling. Gently pinch the pastry, just above the filling, to seal without splitting.
4 Place the parcels onto the prepared baking sheets and drizzle with some of the remaining melted butter. Bake in the oven for about 15 minutes, or until crisp and golden brown.

Chef's tip If using cottage cheese, drain it thoroughly and press the cheese through a sieve before using.

Crudités

A colorful selection of crunchy fresh vegetables served with a choice of dipping sauces is an ideal summer dish for health-conscious guests.

*Preparation time **35 minutes** +*
  1 hour chilling
*Total cooking time **None***
Serves 8–10

SOUR CREAM DIP
1 cup sour cream
2 tablespoons mayonnaise
1/4 cup grated Parmesan
1 teaspoon lime or lemon juice
1/2 teaspoon Worcestershire sauce
1 teaspoon bottled horseradish
1/2 teaspoon Dijon mustard
1/4 teaspoon celery salt

1 English cucumber
2 stalks celery
1 red bell pepper
1 yellow bell pepper
1 small stalk broccoli
12 fresh or 13 oz. canned baby corn
1 cup snow peas
12 baby carrots
20 cherry tomatoes

HERB DIP
2 tablespoons Dijon mustard
1/3 cup red wine vinegar
1 cup olive oil
1/2 tablespoon each of chopped fresh chives, basil,
  parsley and tarragon

1 To prepare the sour cream dip, combine all the ingredients in a bowl and mix well. Chill for at least 1 hour before serving.

2 With a fork, scrape down the length of the cucumber to create a ridged pattern, then cut into 1/4-inch slices. Cut the celery and peppers into 2–3-inch-long sticks. Blanch the broccoli, corn, snow peas and carrots in boiling water for 1 minute. Drain, refresh in cold water and drain again. Remove the broccoli stem and discard. Cut the bushy green part into bite-size pieces. Arrange all the vegetables on a serving platter. Cover with damp paper towels, then wrap in plastic wrap and refrigerate until ready to serve.

3 To prepare the herb dip, place the mustard in a bowl and whisk in the vinegar. Gradually whisk in the oil before adding the herbs and seasoning with salt and freshly ground black pepper. Serve the vegetables with the dips on the side.

Shrimp gougères

Traditionally, a gougère is a round or ring-shaped cheese choux pastry. This variation uses plain choux pastry to make small puffs that are filled with a cold shrimp and mayonnaise mixture.

*Preparation time **40 minutes***
*Total cooking time **25 minutes***
Makes about 20

3 tablespoons unsalted butter, cut into small pieces
pinch of ground nutmeg
2/3 cup all-purpose flour
2 eggs, lightly beaten
I beaten egg, for glazing
8 oz. cooked and shelled shrimp (see Chef's tip)
1/2 cup mayonnaise
I tablespoon finely chopped fresh chives

1 Preheat the oven to 350°F and lightly butter two baking sheets.
2 To make the choux pastry, place 1/2 cup water, the butter, nutmeg and a pinch of salt in a saucepan and bring to a boil, then add the flour and 2 beaten eggs following the method in the Chef's techniques on page 63.

3 Spoon the choux pastry into a pastry bag fitted with a small plain nozzle. Pipe out small balls of dough the size of walnuts onto the prepared baking sheets, leaving a space of 11/4 inches between each ball. Lightly brush the top of each ball with the beaten egg, being careful not to let any excess egg drip down onto the baking sheets, as this may prevent the balls from rising evenly. Bake in the oven for 30 minutes, or until the balls have puffed up and are golden brown. Remove from the oven and transfer to a wire rack to cool.
4 Coarsely chop the shrimp and place in a bowl, then add the mayonnaise and chopped chives and mix together. Season to taste with salt and freshly ground black pepper. Refrigerate until ready to use.
5 Once the choux balls have cooled, cut in half and remove any soft dough from inside the balls. Fill each ball with a small spoonful of the shrimp mixture. Replace the tops, arrange on a serving platter and serve.

Chef's tip If purchasing unshelled shrimp, you will need to buy about 11/4 lb.

Minted pea and cilantro triangles

Despite being a little time-consuming to prepare, the advantage of these tasty savories is that they can be made in advance and baked in the oven as required. It is worth noting that they are suitable for vegetarians.

*Preparation time **55 minutes + 20 minutes cooling***
*Total cooking time **30 minutes***
Makes 30

sprig of fresh mint
1 1/4 cups fresh shelled peas
1 tablespoon vegetable oil
1 onion, cut into cubes the same size as the peas
2 potatoes, about 5 oz., cooked and mashed
2 teaspoons ground coriander
1 tablespoon chopped fresh cilantro
1 tablespoon finely chopped fresh mint
1 tablespoon lemon juice, to taste
1/4 cup unsalted butter, melted
6 sheets phyllo pastry

1 Place the sprig of mint into a pan of salted water and bring to a boil. When boiling, add the peas and cook for 2 minutes. Pour into a colander to drain, then remove and discard the mint.

2 Heat the oil in a skillet over low heat, add the onion and cook for 7 minutes, or until soft and translucent. Increase the heat to medium, add the peas and potato and stir to combine. Transfer to a small bowl and set aside for about 20 minutes to cool.

3 When cool, stir in the ground coriander, cilantro, chopped mint and lemon juice, then season to taste with salt and black pepper. Preheat the oven to 375°F. Brush two baking sheets with some melted butter.

4 Lay the sheets of phyllo pastry out on a work surface and brush with the melted butter. Cut across each sheet to form five strips, about 3 inches wide. Place 2 tea-spoons of the filling on the corner of one end of each strip. Fold the pastry over diagonally to form a triangle at the end. Then keep on folding diagonally up the strip until you have reached the other end.

5 Place the triangles onto the prepared sheets, brush with a little melted butter and bake for 15 minutes, or until crisp and golden brown.

Chef's tip These triangles can be prepared a day in advance and refrigerated before baking, giving you more time to spend with your guests.

Crab fritters with a lime and yogurt mayonnaise

Warm crab and herb fritters are served here with a light tangy dipping sauce. The yogurt and lime in the sauce provide a refreshing contrast to the richness of the mayonnaise.

*Preparation time **20 minutes***
*Total cooking time **15 minutes***
Makes about 30

LIME AND YOGURT MAYONNAISE
2 teaspoons grated lime rind
¹/2 cup plain yogurt
¹/2 cup mayonnaise
fresh lime juice, to taste

CRAB FRITTERS
8 oz. skinned, boneless white fish fillets, such as cod
 or halibut
1 egg white
¹/4 cup whipping cream
8 oz. cooked white crabmeat
2 tablespoons chopped mixed fresh herbs, such as
 dill weed, chives, parsley and tarragon
3 cups fresh bread crumbs

oil, for deep-frying

1 To make the lime and yogurt mayonnaise, stir the lime rind into the yogurt. Mix in the mayonnaise and lime juice to taste, then season with salt and freshly ground black pepper. Cover with plastic wrap and set aside in the refrigerator.

2 To make the crab fritters, purée the fish fillets in a food processor. Add the egg white and some salt and pepper and process again until well blended. Using the pulse button on the processor, carefully add the cream. Do not overwork or the cream will separate. Transfer the mixture to a large bowl and set inside a larger bowl of ice. Using a large metal spoon or plastic spatula, fold in the crabmeat and mixed herbs. Using two teaspoons, shape the mixture into small ovals, or roll by hand into round balls, about 1¹/4 inches in diameter. Sprinkle the bread crumbs onto a sheet of waxed paper and roll the balls in them to coat each one, using the paper to help attach the crumbs without handling the soft mixture too much.

3 Deep-fry the fritters for 4–6 minutes, following the method in the Chef's techniques on page 63. Season the fritters with salt and serve warm with the lime and yogurt mayonnaise on the side.

Chef's tip Once shaped and coated, the crab fritters can be covered with plastic wrap and refrigerated for up to 24 hours before frying.

Cranberry chicken cups

Delicate, creamy little mouthfuls, quick to prepare and guaranteed to impress.

Preparation time **20 minutes**
Total cooking time **10 minutes**
Makes 26

6 sheets phyllo pastry
2/3 cup unsalted butter, melted
3 skinless, boneless chicken breasts, cooked and cut into 1/2-inch cubes
1 tablespoon cranberry sauce
1/4 cup whipping cream or crème fraîche
2 scallions, finely chopped
1/2 teaspoon finely grated lemon rind
fresh cilantro leaves, to garnish
thin strips of lemon rind, to garnish

1 Preheat the oven to 400°F. Following the method in the Chef's techniques on page 63, lay a sheet of phyllo out on a work surface and brush with the butter. Place a second sheet on top and brush with butter, then repeat to make two stacks, each with three layers of phyllo pastry.

2 Using a round 3-inch cutter, cut 26 disks from the phyllo and, buttered-side-down, press gently into individual fluted tartlet pans about 2 inches across and 3/4-inch-deep.

3 Place small circles of waxed paper into the pastry shells and fill with pie weights or rice. Bake for 10 minutes, or until golden. Remove the weights or rice and paper and cool the pastry in the pans.

4 In a bowl, combine the chicken, cranberry sauce, cream or crème fraîche, scallions, lemon rind and some salt and pepper. Spoon into the tartlet shells and garnish with a cilantro leaf and the lemon rind.

Chef's tip The chicken can be replaced with cooked turkey, duck or flaked smoked trout.

Smoked salmon and trout roulade
on pumpernickel

Pumpernickel, a coarse, dark bread made from a high proportion of rye flour, has a slightly sour taste, which complements the rich creamy taste of the smoked fish topping.

*Preparation time **25 minutes + 30 minutes chilling***
*Total cooking time **None***
Makes 20

4 oz. smoked trout fillet
4 oz. cream cheese
1 tablespoon lemon juice
6 oz. smoked salmon slices
20 slices pumpernickel
sprigs of fresh chervil or parsley, to garnish

1 Remove any skin or bones from the trout and place into a food processor with 3 oz. of the cream cheese. Process until blended and smooth, then season to taste with salt and pepper. Add the lemon juice and process once more to combine.

2 Lay the smoked salmon slices onto a piece of plastic wrap in an 8- x 6-inch rectangular shape, with the edges of the slices overlapping. Spread an even layer of the smoked trout mixture onto the salmon, then roll the slices up from the widest side, like a jelly roll, using the plastic wrap to help lift as you roll. Wrap the salmon and trout roulade in plastic wrap and place it in the freezer for 30 minutes, or until set and firm enough to slice.

3 Using a 2-inch cutter, cut 20 rounds from the pumpernickel. Spread the remaining cream cheese onto the pumpernickel circles. Remove the salmon roulade from the freezer, discard the plastic wrap and cut across the roulade, using a very sharp knife, to make about 20 slices. Top each piece of pumpernickel with a roulade slice and decorate with a sprig of chervil or parsley. Cover with plastic wrap and keep chilled until ready to serve.

Creamed Roquefort and walnuts

These delicious, easily prepared toasts are best made less than 30 minutes in advance to prevent the toast from becoming too soft.

*Preparation time **15 minutes***
*Total cooking time **10 minutes***
Makes 40

¹/₄ cup coarsely chopped walnuts
10 slices whole-grain bread, about ¹/₄-inch thick
2 oz. Roquefort or other strong blue cheese
2 oz. cream cheese
chopped fresh parsley, to garnish

1 Spread the walnuts on a baking sheet and toast them under a preheated broiler for 3–5 minutes, shaking the sheet frequently to ensure that they are evenly browned and do not burn. Alternatively, toast the nuts for 7–10 minutes in the oven at 350°F. Set aside to cool.
2 Cut the bread slices into 1¹/₂-inch circles using a plain round cutter. Toast lightly on both sides using the broiler, then set aside.
3 In a small bowl, break up the Roquefort using a fork, add the cream cheese and mix well. Stir in half the chopped walnuts, then spread the mixture onto each round of toast. Sprinkle the remaining chopped walnuts and some chopped parsley onto the cheese mixture to decorate. Serve immediately.

Crostini of roasted peppers and basil

The name crostini comes from the Italian word crosta, *meaning "crust." Crostini are small rounds of toasted bread with toppings such as pâté, cheese or, as in this case, roasted vegetables.*

*Preparation time **25 minutes***
*Total cooking time **10 minutes***
Makes 12

¹/₂ small red bell pepper, cut in half
¹/₂ small green bell pepper, cut in half
2 tablespoons shredded fresh basil
¹/₄ cup olive oil
¹/₂ French baguette (preferably stale)
I clove garlic
Parmesan shavings, to garnish

1 Preheat the oven to 400°F. To broil the peppers, follow the method in the Chef's techniques on page 62.
2 Cut the peppers into thin strips and put them into a bowl with the basil and 1 tablespoon of the olive oil, or just enough to bind the mixture. Season with salt and freshly ground black pepper
3 Cut the baguette into slices ⁵/₈-inch thick. Toast the slices on both sides under a preheated broiler or in a toaster, then brush them with the remaining oil. Rub the garlic clove over the crostini and spoon some of the roasted pepper mixture onto each one. Serve immediately, topped with the Parmesan shavings.

Creamed Roquefort and walnuts (top) and Crostini of roasted pepper and basil

Mini blinis with caviar

Brightly colored and extremely appetizing, these small pancakes topped with sour cream and caviar or roe are bound to disappear very quickly.

Preparation time **45 minutes + 30 minutes resting**
Total cooking time **35 minutes**
Makes 40–45

¹/₄ oz. fresh yeast or ¹/₈ oz. dried yeast
²/₃ cup milk, lukewarm
2 teaspoons sugar
¹/₂ cup all-purpose flour
¹/₂ cup buckwheat flour
2 eggs, separated
3 tablespoons butter, melted but cooled
sour cream, to garnish
caviar or lumpfish roe, to garnish
sprigs of fresh dill weed or chervil, to garnish

1 Dissolve the yeast in the lukewarm milk, then mix in the sugar, flours, egg yolks and a large pinch of salt. Cover and set aside to rest for 30 minutes in a warm place. After resting, the batter should be foamy and thick. Mix in the melted butter.

2 Beat the egg whites with a pinch of salt until soft peaks form. Gently fold into the batter.

3 Over medium heat, melt a little butter in a nonstick skillet. Using a small spoon, place dollops of the batter in the pan, trying to make them as uniform as possible and being careful not to overcrowd them. Once the batter begins to set around the edges and the surface is bubbly, carefully flip the blinis over. Cook for another 2–3 minutes, or until brown. Transfer to a wire rack to cool (you can overlap them, but do not stack). Repeat until all the batter has been used.

4 If necessary, use a small round cutter to trim the blinis to the same size. Lay on a serving platter and place a spoon of sour cream in the center and top with some caviar or roe. Finish with a sprig of dill weed or chervil.

Chef's tips If you have any fresh yeast left over, it can be stored in the refrigerator, lightly wrapped in waxed paper, for up to 2 weeks.

Other types of popular caviar appropriate for this recipe include salmon or red caviar.

Potato and smoked fish croquettes

Deliciously crisp, golden brown potato croquettes flavored with smoked fish and garlic, which can be served with the sauce of your choice, whether a tomato sauce, garlic mayonnaise or salsa.

Preparation time **30 minutes + 15 minutes chilling**
Total cooking time **45 minutes**
Makes 40

1 lb. baking potatoes, such as Idaho or russet
1 tablespoon unsalted butter
1 egg yolk
pinch of ground nutmeg
1 tablespoon olive oil
2 cloves garlic, crushed
1/3 cup whipping cream
5 oz. boneless smoked haddock, trout or salmon,
   crumbled or thinly sliced
1/2 cup all-purpose flour
3 eggs, beaten
1 tablespoon peanut oil
2 cups fresh bread crumbs
oil, for deep-frying

1 Cut the peeled potatoes into uniform pieces for even cooking. Place them in a medium saucepan, cover with cold water and add a large pinch of salt. Bring to a boil, lower the heat and simmer for at least 20 minutes, or until they are quite tender.

2 Drain the potatoes and dry them by shaking them in their pan over a low heat. Press them through a sieve or finely mash and add the butter, egg yolk, nutmeg and some salt and pepper. Place the mixture into a large bowl to cool.

3 Heat the olive oil in a saucepan, add the garlic and cook for 1 minute to soften. Stir in the cream and simmer until reduced by half. Add the fish to the potato mixture with the reduced cream. Season with salt and pepper and mix to combine well.

4 Season the flour with salt and pepper and place in a shallow dish. Place the beaten eggs and peanut oil into a shallow bowl and the bread crumbs onto a large piece of waxed paper. Shape the potato mixture into ovals about 1 1/2 x 3/4 inches in size and roll each one carefully in the flour, patting off the excess. Dip them in the egg mixture, then drain off the excess and roll them in the bread crumbs, lifting the edges of the paper to help you. Sometimes it is necessary to coat the croquettes twice in the egg and bread crumbs, especially if your mixture is a little too soft to hold its shape well. Refrigerate for 15 minutes.

5 Heat the oil in a deep-fat fryer or deep saucepan (see Chef's techniques, page 63). Deep-fry, in batches, for 3–4 minutes, or until golden brown. Lift out, draining off excess oil, and drain on crumpled paper towels. Serve the croquettes with a sauce and lime wedges.

Chef's tip The potato must not be too wet or the moisture will cause the croquettes to split and absorb the oil. Using bread crumbs on a large piece of paper enables you to coat the croquettes without too much mess. Always shake off or press on excess bread crumbs or they will fall into the oil when frying, burn and then cling to the croquettes as unsightly specks.

Smoked salmon pancake rolls

One of the attractive features of this recipe, which successfully combines the flavors of smoked salmon and horseradish, is that the pancakes may be prepared in advance and frozen.

*Preparation time **1 hour + 15 minutes resting***
   + 1 hour refrigeration
*Total cooking time **10 minutes***
*Makes **30–35***

PANCAKE DOUGH
1 cup all-purpose flour
2 teaspoons sesame oil

5 oz. cream cheese, at room
   temperature
1 tablespoon bottled horseradish
1/2 teaspoon lemon juice
6 oz. smoked salmon slices
chopped fresh chives or herbs, to garnish

1 To make the pancake dough, bring 1/3 cup water to a boil, add the flour, roll out the dough and brush with the oil and cook, following the method for preparing pancakes in the Chef's techniques on page 62. Stack the pancakes on a plate and keep them wrapped in a slightly damp cloth to prevent them from drying out.

2 Soften the cream cheese in a small bowl and mix with the horseradish and lemon juice until smooth.

3 Place a pancake on a work surface and trim off the upper third of the circle. Spread with a thin layer of the cheese mixture, then cover with a layer of salmon. Roll up as tightly as possible. Wrap in plastic wrap to keep it from unrolling and set aside. Repeat with the remaining pancakes. Refrigerate for at least 1 hour.

4 Just before serving, trim the ends of each roll, then slice into 5/8-inch pieces and pierce with a toothpick. Scatter a few chives or fresh herbs in the center of each roll, arrange on a platter and serve.

Chef's tip The pancakes may be prepared ahead of time and frozen. Briefly steam to soften before using.

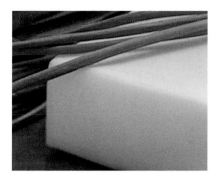

Blue cheese puffs

Any type of blue cheese, such as Stilton or the creamy Italian Dolcelatte, may be used to make these puffs. However, if you use the strong salty Roquefort cheese, omit the salt in the recipe.

Preparation time **10 minutes**
Total cooking time **25 minutes**
Makes about 55

CREAM-PUFF PASTRY
¹/₃ cup unsalted butter
3/4 cup bread or all-purpose flour
2 eggs, beaten

3 oz. blue cheese, shredded or mashed
pinch of dry mustard, optional
oil, for deep-frying
finely chopped fresh chives, to garnish

1 To make the cream-puff pastry, melt the butter and ³/4 cup water in a large saucepan over low heat, then add the flour and eggs, following the method in the Chef's techniques on page 63. Stir in the blue cheese and season to taste with salt, freshly ground black pepper and the dry mustard if desired.

2 Heat the oil in a deep-fat fryer or deep saucepan (see Chef's techniques, page 63). Using two lightly oiled teaspoons, scoop out a small amount of the mixture with one and push off with the other spoon to carefully lower into the hot oil. Cook the mixture in batches until puffed, golden brown and crisp, turning with a long-handled metal spoon to ensure even coloring. Drain on crumpled paper towels.

3 Sprinkle the warm puffs lightly with the chives and serve immediately.

Chef's tips The puff mixture may be prepared in advance, covered with plastic wrap and refrigerated for a few hours before deep-frying.

Dolcelatte is also known as Gorgonzola dolce.

Corn and chicken fritters

*Golden kernels of juicy sweet corn with the
distinctive flavor of cilantro and soy sauce
make these fritters irresistible.*

*Preparation time **20 minutes + refrigeration***
*Total cooking time **45 minutes***
Makes about 65

2 eggs, lightly beaten
2 x 14 oz. cans corn kernels, well drained
1/4 cup cornstarch
**12 oz. skinless, boneless chicken breast halves,
   finely chopped**
2 tablespoons chopped fresh cilantro
1 tablespoon sugar
1 tablespoon soy sauce
oil, for frying

1 In a large bowl, combine the eggs, corn kernels,
cornstarch, chicken, cilantro, sugar and soy sauce and
mix well. Cover and leave to chill in the refrigerator for
at least 1 hour, or overnight if possible.
2 In a large skillet, heat 1/8 inch oil. Using a tablespoon,
drop in enough corn mixture to make 1 1/4-inch circles,
taking care not to crowd the pan. Fry for 3 minutes, or
until golden, then turn over to brown the second side.
Lift out and drain on crumpled paper towels. Repeat
with the remaining mixture, adding more oil to the pan
when necessary. Serve the fritters warm.

Chef's tips Make the first fritter a small one, taste to
check the seasoning and, if necessary, add salt and
pepper to the mixture before cooking the rest.
   These fritters are delicious topped with some plain
yogurt and a drizzle of sweet chili sauce.

Cheese palm leaves

*These small pastry savories are delicious served with cocktails or soups. They can either
be shaped as palm leaves or as the twisted sticks known as cheese straws.*

Preparation time **30 minutes + 45 minutes refrigeration**
Total cooking time **10 minutes**
Makes 40

2 egg yolks
I egg
1/4 teaspoon sugar
melted butter, for brushing
3/4 cup grated Parmesan
1/2 teaspoon paprika
I sheet pre-rolled frozen puff pastry, thawed

1 Beat together the egg yolks, egg, sugar and about
1/4 teaspoon salt and strain into a clean bowl.
2 Brush two baking sheets with melted butter and
place in the refrigerator. In a bowl, combine the
Parmesan, paprika, 1/2 teaspoon salt and some freshly
ground black pepper.
3 On a lightly floured surface, roll out the pastry sheet
and trim to a 12-inch square. Cut the square in half,
brush both halves lightly with the egg mixture and
sprinkle with the Parmesan mixture. Using the rolling
pin, press the cheese mixture into the pastry. Carefully
slide the pastry sheets onto two trays and refrigerate for
15 minutes.

4 Transfer the pastry sheets to a lightly floured surface
and trim back to 12- x 6-inch rectangles. With the back
of a knife, lightly mark each pastry into 2-inch-wide
strips, parallel to the short ends. Sprinkle with a
little water.
5 Fold the two outer strips of each sheet inwards over
the next strip. Their non-cheese undersides will now be
on the top. Brush with a little water and fold over onto
the next marked strips, brush with water again and fold
into a neat stack. Transfer to a tray and chill for
15 minutes. Cut the stacks crosswise into 1/4-inch slices
and place, cut-side-down and well apart, on the
prepared baking sheets. Press to lightly flatten, turn over
and chill for 15 minutes.
6 Meanwhile, preheat the oven to 400°F. Bake the
palm leaves for 8 minutes, or until golden and crisp.
Remove to a wire rack to cool.

Chef's tips To make cheese straws, use the same
ingredients and follow the method for steps 1–3. Cut
1/2-inch-wide strips from the pastry sheets and twist
each several times to form a long, loose ringlet. Lay on
the baking sheets and press both ends down firmly. Chill
for about 15 minutes, then bake for 12–15 minutes, or
until golden. Immediately cut each straw into 4-inch
lengths and remove to a wire rack to cool.

Roquefort in Belgian endive leaves

The butter used in this recipe helps to soften both the texture and the distinctive salty taste of the Roquefort, a blue-vein sheep's milk cheese from southern France.

*Preparation time **20 minutes***
*Total cooking time **None***
Makes 40–45

8 oz. Roquefort or other strong blue cheese
1/2 cup unsalted butter, at room temperature
1 tablespoon port or Madeira
4 Belgian endives
2 tablespoons chopped walnuts
a few sprigs of fresh parsley, to garnish

1 Place the cheese, butter and port in a food processor and process until smooth. Season to taste with freshly ground black pepper and more port if desired. Transfer to a bowl and set aside.

2 Remove any damaged outer leaves from the endives and discard. Cut about 1/4 inch from the bottom and carefully remove all the loose leaves. Repeat until all the leaves are loose.

3 Put the cheese mixture into a pastry bag fitted with a medium star nozzle and pipe a small rosette of cheese at the bottom of each endive leaf. Sprinkle with some chopped walnuts, then arrange on a round platter with the tips of the leaves pointing outward like the petals of a flower. Form the parsley into a bouquet and place in the center. Serve immediately.

Chef's tip The cheese filling may be prepared ahead of time and stored, covered with plastic wrap, in the refrigerator; but once the endive is cut, it tends to discolor, so prepare the leaves just before serving.

Spiced shrimp balls

The fried sesame seeds enclosing the tasty shrimp mixture will give a strong, distinctive flavor and a lovely golden brown color to these delicious savory snacks.

Preparation time **15 minutes + 20 minutes chilling**
Total cooking time **15 minutes**
Makes 24

1 1/2 lb. large raw shrimp
1 tablespoon oil
2 cloves garlic, crushed
1/2-inch piece fresh ginger root, finely chopped
1/4 teaspoon salt
2 teaspoons sugar
1 teaspoon chopped fresh cilantro
1 teaspoon cornstarch
1/2 egg white
2/3 cup sesame seeds
oil, for deep-frying

1 Remove the shells from the shrimp. Take each shrimp and make a shallow cut along the back with a small knife, then carefully pull out the dark vein with the tip of the knife. Pat dry with paper towels.

2 Put the shrimp in a food processor and process to a coarse purée. Transfer to a bowl and add the oil, garlic, ginger root, salt, sugar, cilantro and cornstarch and mix well to combine.

3 Lightly whisk the egg white until it just stands in soft peaks, then add just enough of the egg white to the spiced shrimp mixture to obtain a smooth, stiff mixture that will hold a shape.

4 Divide the mixture into 24 evenly sized balls. Roll them in the sesame seeds to coat, set them on a baking sheet and chill in the refrigerator for 20 minutes.

5 Heat the oil in a deep-fat fryer or deep saucepan (see Chef's techniques, page 63). Cook the balls in three batches, for about 4–5 minutes, or until they are golden brown and crispy on the outside and cooked through. Drain on crumpled paper towels. Arrange them on a serving plate and serve hot.

Cornish pasties

In the eighteenth and nineteenth centuries, Cornish pasties were taken down into the mines by miners and eaten as a complete meal. There was meat at one end and apple or jam at the other, with scrolled initials in the pastry to indicate the difference. This recipe, however, is for modern savory pasties that have been miniaturized and adapted to be served as finger food.

Preparation time **35 minutes + 30 minutes chilling**
Total cooking time **30 minutes**
Makes 48

PASTRY
4 cups all-purpose flour
pinch of salt
3/4 cup unsalted butter, cut into
  cubes and chilled
1/4 cup lard, cut into cubes and chilled
8 tablespoons water

FILLING
1 potato, about 3 oz., coarsely chopped
1/4 rutabaga, about 3 oz., coarsely chopped
1 tablespoon unsalted butter
1/2 onion, finely chopped
4 oz. lean ground beef
2 oz. beef kidney, finely chopped,
  optional

melted butter, for brushing
milk, for brushing

1 To make the pastry, sift the flour and salt into a large bowl and add the butter and lard. Using a fast, light, flicking action of thumb across fingertips, rub the butter and lard into the flour until the mixture resembles fine bread crumbs. Make a well, add 1 tablespoon of the water and mix with a round-bladed knife until small lumps form. Continue to add the tablespoons of water,

making a different well for each one and only using the last tablespoon if necessary. When the mixture is in large lumps, pick up and lightly press together. Knead the pastry on a lightly floured surface until just smooth. Wrap in plastic wrap and chill in the refrigerator for 20 minutes. Brush two baking sheets with melted butter and set aside.

2 To make the filling, put the potato and rutabaga into a food processor and, using the pulse button, finely chop but do not purée. Melt the butter in a skillet, add the onion and cook gently for 4 minutes. Add the potato and rutabaga, turn the heat up to medium and cook for about 2 minutes, stirring occasionally, until just tender. Add the beef and kidney, turn the heat to high and fry, stirring constantly, for 5 minutes. Drain off the excess fat, season well with salt and pepper and leave to cool.

3 Cut the pastry in half and on a lightly floured surface, roll out each half 1/8 inch thick. Cut out about 24 circles, using a 2 1/2-inch round cutter, from each half of pastry, and place 1 teaspoon of the filling on one side, 1/4 inch from the edge. Moisten the edge with water and fold the unfilled side over to form a semicircle, pressing the edges together well to seal. Using a fork, press down on the edge of the pastries to form a decorative pattern. With the point of a knife, twist to make a small steam vent on top of each pastry and lay them on the prepared baking sheets. Place in the refrigerator to chill for 10 minutes.

4 Preheat the oven to 400°F. Using a pastry brush, brush the top of the pasties with a little milk and bake in the oven for 15 minutes, or until the pasties are golden brown.

Saté beef sticks

Widely cooked throughout Southeast Asia, a saté consists of marinated meat, fish or poultry, threaded onto bamboo or wooden skewers, broiled or barbecued, and served with a sauce.

Preparation time **35 minutes + 2–3 hours marinating**
Total cooking time **15 minutes**
Makes 20

1/4 teaspoon ground aniseed
1/4 teaspoon ground cumin
1 teaspoon ground turmeric
1 teaspoon ground coriander
1 shallot, chopped
1 clove garlic, finely chopped
1/2 inch piece of fresh ginger root, finely chopped
1 stalk lemon grass, white part only, finely chopped
1 tablespoon brown sugar
2 tablespoons peanut oil
1 teaspoon soy sauce
6 oz. beef tenderloin, cut into 20 thin strips

SATE SAUCE
1 clove garlic
1/3 cup smooth peanut butter
3 tablespoons coconut milk
a few drops of Tabasco, or to taste
2 teaspoons honey
2 teaspoons lemon juice
2 teaspoons light soy sauce

1 Soak 20 short wooden skewers in water for 1 hour to prevent them burning under the broiler. To make the marinade, add the ground aniseed, cumin, turmeric and coriander to the shallot, garlic, ginger, lemon grass and brown sugar in a medium bowl. Mix well and add the oil and soy sauce.

2 Thread a strip of beef onto each wooden skewer (see Chef's techniques, page 62) and place in a shallow dish. Thoroughly coat in the marinade and refrigerate for 2–3 hours.

3 To make the saté sauce, put the garlic into a small saucepan and cover with cold water. Bring to a boil and simmer for 3 minutes, refresh under cold water, then drain and finely chop. Combine the garlic with the peanut butter, coconut milk and 1/4 cup water in a medium saucepan. Stir over medium heat for 1–2 minutes, or until smooth and thick, then add the Tabasco, honey, lemon juice and soy sauce. Stir until the sauce is warm and thoroughly blended. If the mixture starts to separate, stir in 1–2 teaspoons water. Cover with plastic wrap and place in the refrigerator until ready to use.

4 Preheat a broiler or barbecue until hot. Cook the beef saté sticks for 1–2 minutes on each side, turning three or four times during cooking. Once they are cooked, arrange on a plate and serve with the saté sauce.

Welsh rarebit

Originally called Welsh rabbit, the name of these toasted cheese slices was changed to Welsh rarebit in the eighteenth century. It has been speculated that rarebit was originally "rearbit," because these treats were served at the end of a meal.

Preparation time **15 minutes**
Total cooking time **4 minutes**
Makes 16

¹/₂ **cup grated Gruyère cheese**
¹/₂ **cup grated Cheddar**
I teaspoon French mustard
pinch of cayenne pepper
I egg, beaten
I tablespoon beer
4 slices bread
I tablespoon unsalted butter, at room temperature
chopped fresh parsley, to garnish

1 Preheat the broiler. Mix the Gruyère and Cheddar together, stir in the mustard and cayenne pepper and season with salt and black pepper. Mix in the beaten egg and beer and set aside.

2 Remove the crusts from the bread and toast the slices on both sides. Immediately spread one side of each slice with the butter. Spoon the cheese mixture on to the toast and spread neatly, making sure that all the edges are covered.

3 Place under the broiler for 3–4 minutes, or until the cheese mixture is bubbling and lightly browned. Remove and immediately cut each slice into four fingers or triangles. Sprinkle with the chopped parsley and serve hot.

Shrimp toast

These are quick and easy to prepare and can be cut into any shape. They must be served warm.

Preparation time **20 minutes + 30 minutes refrigeration**
Total cooking time **15 minutes**
Makes about 40

12 shelled and deveined large raw shrimp,
  about 12 oz.
2 teaspoons sherry
¹/₂ **teaspoon salt**
¹/₂ **teaspoon pepper**
2 teaspoons sesame oil
2 egg whites
2¹/₂ **tablespoons cornstarch**
1¹/₂ **tablespoons chopped fresh cilantro**
2 scallions, finely chopped
10 slices bread
whole fresh cilantro leaves, to garnish
oil, for deep-frying

1 In a food processor, process the shrimp until finely chopped. Add the sherry, salt, pepper, sesame oil, egg whites and cornstarch. Process until smooth, then stir in the chopped cilantro and scallions.

2 Remove the crusts from the bread slices. Spread on a layer of shrimp purée, half the thickness of the bread, all the way to the edges. Refrigerate for 30 minutes, or until the purée is firm. Cut the bread into squares, triangles or rectangles and smooth the cut edges if necessary. Press a cilantro leaf onto each shape.

3 Heat the oil in a deep-fat fryer or deep saucepan (see Chef's techniques, page 63). Deep-fry the shrimp toasts in batches for 2–3 minutes, or until golden brown. Remove with a slotted spoon and drain on crumpled paper towels. Serve immediately.

Welsh rarebit (top) and Shrimp toast

Melting morsels

As the name suggests, these rich cheese pastries melt in the mouth. They may be prepared up to a week in advance as they keep well if stored in an airtight container in a cool place.

Preparation time **35 minutes + 50 minutes chilling**
Total cooking time **10 minutes per tray**
Makes 64

melted butter, for brushing
3/4 cup all-purpose flour
pinch of celery salt
1/3 cup unsalted butter, cut into cubes and chilled
2/3 cup grated Cheddar
2 tablespoons grated Parmesan
1 egg yolk
1 egg, beaten
1 tablespoon finely grated Parmesan,
  for the topping

1 Preheat the oven to 375°F. Brush two baking sheets with melted butter and refrigerate.
2 Sift the flour, celery salt and a pinch of salt and freshly ground black pepper together into a medium bowl. Add the butter cubes and, using two round-bladed knives, cut the mixture from the center to the edges of the bowl with a quick action.
3 When the flour has almost disappeared into the butter, add the Cheddar and Parmesan and continue cutting for a few moments more until the mixture is blended and coming together in rough lumps. Make a well in the center and cut in the egg yolk until combined. Gather together by hand to form a ball.
4 Wrap the dough loosely in plastic wrap and flatten slightly. Chill for about 20 minutes until firm.
5 Place the dough on a lightly floured work surface. Cut in half and roll out each half to an 8-inch square, 1/4 inch thick. Cut each square into 16 small squares, then cut each square in half to form triangles. Using a flexible metal spatula, carefully place enough triangles to comfortably fill the two baking sheets, and chill for 30 minutes.
6 Brush each triangle with beaten egg and sprinkle with a pinch of the extra Parmesan. Bake for 10 minutes, or until golden brown. Place on a wire rack to cool. Repeat with the remaining mixture, preparing the baking sheets as instructed in step 1.

Chef's tip If you want, you can try varying the topping by sprinkling with finely chopped nuts and sea salt, poppy seeds or some grated Parmesan mixed with a pinch of cayenne.

Mini brochettes

It is important to marinate the ingredients as this will bring more flavor to the brochettes and make sure that the meat is deliciously tender.

Preparation time **25 minutes + 1 hour marinating**
Total cooking time **15 minutes**
Makes 20

3/4 cup veal or chicken stock
2 cloves garlic, crushed
2 teaspoons chopped fresh ginger root
2 tablespoons dark soy sauce
2 teaspoons sesame oil
1 skinless, boneless chicken breast half, cut into
   1/2-inch cubes
1/2 red bell pepper, cut into 1/2-inch cubes
1/2 yellow bell pepper, cut into 1/2-inch cubes
2 scallions, sliced diagonally
1 teaspoon cornstarch

1 Soak 20 short wooden skewers in water for 1 hour to prevent them from burning during cooking. Pour the stock into a saucepan and simmer until it has reduced by a third and is syrupy. In a bowl, combine the reduced stock with the garlic, ginger root, soy sauce and sesame oil. Leave to cool.

2 Thread alternating pieces of chicken, red and yellow pepper and scallion onto the skewers. Place the brochettes in a flat dish and season. Pour half the cooled marinade over the brochettes. Cover with plastic wrap and refrigerate for at least 1 hour.

3 To make the dipping sauce, heat the remaining marinade in a small saucepan, then mix the cornstarch with a little water and stir in until the sauce boils and thickens. Set aside and keep warm.

4 Preheat the broiler or barbecue. Drain the brochettes and cook for 3 minutes, turning, until the meat is cooked. Serve immediately with the dipping sauce.

Parma ham and melon fingers

An extremely refreshing all-time favorite that is best made with paper-thin slices of Parma ham or prosciutto.

Preparation time **10 minutes**
Total cooking time **None**
Makes 32

I small cantaloupe
II slices Parma ham or prosciutto

1 Cut the melon in half lengthwise and, using a spoon, remove the seeds and gently scrape clean. Slice each half into eight wedges.
2 With a sharp knife, starting at one end of a melon wedge, slice between the flesh and the thick rind of the melon. Cut each piece of peeled melon in half.
3 Cut each slice of Parma ham or prosciutto into three long strips.
4 Wrap a strip of Parma ham or prosciutto around each wedge of melon and secure with a cocktail pick.

Marinated fish and tapenade on toast

Tapenade, a simple spread from Provence in France, is made by puréeing black olives, anchovies, capers, olive oil and lemon juice.

Preparation time **10 minutes + 15 minutes marinating**
Total cooking time **10 minutes**
Makes 16

2 fillets, about 6 oz. goat fish or other firm, lean white fish, skinned and boned
I clove garlic
2 tablespoons olive oil
4 slices bread, crusts removed
1/3 cup tapenade
16 pink peppercorns
16 sprigs of fresh dill weed
small wedges of lemon, to garnish

1 Preheat the oven to 425°F. Cut each fish fillet into eight pieces. Place the garlic clove in the olive oil, toss into the fish and leave to marinate for 15 minutes.
2 Toast the bread and spread with a thin layer of tapenade. Cut each slice diagonally into four triangles and arrange on a baking sheet. Place the marinated fish on the prepared toasts and, just before serving, place in the oven for 2–3 minutes, or until the fish is just cooked (it will flake when lightly pressed with a fork).
3 Remove from the oven and transfer to a serving tray. Place a small dot of the tapenade on the top, then a pink peppercorn in the center. Decorate with a sprig of dill weed and a lemon wedge.

Chef's tips Red mullet goes particularly well with this recipe, but can be difficult to obtain. Check with your local fish merchant for availability.

Tapenade is available ready-made from gourmet delicatessens.

Spring rolls with pork stuffing

These rolls are deep-fried, however, if you do not have a deep-fat fryer, it is possible to use a heavy-bottomed saucepan. The results will be just as good, but extreme care should be taken with the hot oil.

Preparation time *40 minutes + 30 minutes chilling*
Total cooking time *40 minutes*
Makes about 40

2 tablespoons oil
8 oz. lean ground pork
¹/₂ Chinese cabbage, finely shredded (see page 63)
2 scallions, sliced
I teaspoon grated fresh ginger root
2 tablespoons finely chopped bamboo shoots
3 button mushrooms, thinly sliced
¹/₂ teaspoon dried sage
I teaspoon soy sauce
2 teaspoons cornstarch
20 spring roll wrappers, about 8 inches square
soy sauce, to serve

1 Heat the oil in a large skillet over high heat, add the pork and cook for about 3 minutes, stirring constantly. Transfer the meat to a bowl to cool. When cool, add the Chinese cabbage, scallions, ginger root, bamboo shoots, mushrooms, dried sage, soy sauce and 1 teaspoon of the cornstarch. Stir to combine well, then season to taste with salt and pepper.

2 Add a little water to the remaining teaspoon of cornstarch to make a paste and set aside. Prepare the spring rolls by following the method in the Chef's techniques on page 63. Place in the refrigerator to chill for at least 30 minutes before cooking.

3 Heat the oil in a deep-fat fryer or deep saucepan (see Chef's techniques, page 63). Fry the spring rolls in batches of four or five for about 3–5 minutes, or until cooked and golden brown. The spring rolls will float to the surface of the oil when cooked. Remove and drain on crumpled paper towels. Serve the spring rolls hot with the soy sauce.

Chef's tip These could also be made using phyllo pastry. Brush sheets of phyllo with melted butter (as directed on page 11), wrap around the filling, then bake in a 400°F oven for 10 minutes, or until golden and crisp.

Chef's techniques

◆

Preparing pancakes

These pancakes can be made with any moist filling, such as herbed cream cheese and smoked fish.

Using a fork or chopsticks, slowly incorporate the flour into the water until a soft dough forms. Turn out onto a floured surface and knead for 5 minutes, or until smooth. Cover and set aside for 15 minutes.

Divide the dough into six and roll into balls. Flatten one ball, brush lightly with some sesame oil and place another flattened round of dough on top. Roll out into 8¹/₂-inch circles, about ¹/₁₆-inch thick.

Heat a dry skillet over medium-high heat. Place a pancake in the hot pan and cook for 50–60 seconds, or until blistered and colored. Flip over and cook for another 30–40 seconds.

Transfer the pancake to a plate and, while it is still hot, carefully peel it apart, being careful of any hot steam. Repeat with the remaining pancakes.

Broiling peppers

Broiling peppers allows you to remove their skins and produces a delicious sweet flavor.

Preheat a broiler. Cut the peppers in half and remove the seeds and membrane.

Broil the peppers until the skin blisters and blackens. Place in a plastic food bag and allow to cool. When cool, peel off the skin.

Threading saté beef

This is an attractive way to present satés, although the meat can also be cut into small cubes.

If using wooden skewers, soak in cold water for about 1 hour before using to prevent them from burning. Cut the beef into ¹/₄-inch strips. Thread onto wooden skewers.

Choux pastry

Little balls of light choux pastry can be filled or sandwiched together with savory or sweet fillings.

Once the butter has melted, bring to a boil, then add all the flour and stir constantly with a wooden spoon until the mixture rolls off the side of the pan. Remove from the heat and cool until just warm.

Transfer the mixture to a medium bowl. Add the egg in six additions, beating well between each addition until the mixture thickens.

Rolling up spring rolls

Spring roll wrappers are very delicate and should be covered with a damp cloth while you work.

Shred the cabbage leaves by rolling them up tightly and cutting finely.

Cut each spring roll wrapper in half. Divide the filling among all the wrappers and roll up tightly. Seal the edges using cornstarch paste.

Layering phyllo pastry

Purchased phyllo is very easy to use as long as you keep it covered to prevent it from drying out.

Place the sheets of phyllo pastry on a work surface and cover with a damp dish towel. Work with one sheet at a time, keeping the rest covered to stop them from drying out.

Brush the first sheet with melted butter, then place another sheet on top and brush again with melted butter. Repeat until you have the number of layers specified in the recipe.

Deep-frying

Fill the fryer one-third full of oil; do not leave it unattended. Dry food thoroughly before deep-frying.

Preheat the oil in a deep-fat fryer or deep saucepan to 350°F. Place a bread cube in the oil: If it sizzles and turns golden brown in 15 seconds, the oil is hot enough.

First published in the United States in 1998 by Periplus Editions (HK) Ltd., with editorial offices at
153 Milk Street, Boston, Massachusetts 02109.

Murdoch Books and Le Cordon Bleu thank the 32 masterchefs of all the Le Cordon Bleu Schools, whose knowledge and expertise have made this book possible, especially: Chef Cliche (MOF), Chef Terrien, Chef Boucheret, Chef Duchêne (MOF), Chef Guillut, Chef Steneck, Paris; Chef Males, Chef Walsh, Chef Hardy, London; Chef Chantefort, Chef Bertin, Chef Jambert, Chef Honda, Tokyo; Chef Salembien, Chef Boutin, Chef Harris, Sydney; Chef Lawes, Adelaide; Chef Guiet, Chef Denis, Ottawa. Of the many students who helped the Chefs test each recipe, a special mention to graduates David Welch and Allen Wertheim. A very special acknowledgment to Directors Susan Eckstein, Great Britain, and Kathy Shaw, Paris, who have been responsible for the coordination of the Le Cordon Bleu team throughout this series.

The Publisher and Le Cordon Bleu also wish to thank Carole Sweetnam for her help with this series.

First published in Australia in 1998 by Murdoch Books®

Managing Editor: Kay Halsey
Series Concept, Design and Art Direction: Juliet Cohen
Food Director: Jody Vassallo
Food Editors: Kathy Knudsen, Tracy Rutherford
US Editor: Linda Venturoni Wilson
Designer: Annette Fitzgerald
Photographer: André Martin
Food Stylist: Jane Hann
Food Preparation: Alison Turner
Chef's Techniques Photographer: Reg Morrison
Home Economists: Kathy Knudsen, Justine Poole, Zoe Radze, Alison Turner

Library of Congress catalog card number: 98-85717
ISBN 962-593-444-8

Front cover: Spinach and feta parcels

Distributed in the United States by
Tuttle Publishing
Distribution Center
Airport Industrial Park
364 Innovation Drive
North Clarendon, VT 05759-9436
Tel: (802) 773-8930
Fax: (802) 773-6993

Printed in Singapore

05 04 03 02 01   10 9 8 7 6 5 4 3 2

Important: Some of the recipes in this book may include raw eggs, which can cause salmonella poisoning. Those who might be at risk from this (the elderly, pregnant women, young children and those suffering from immune deficiency diseases) should check with their physicians before eating raw eggs.